(Insurance) Makes Cents

The Art of Money Well ~~Spent~~ Wasted

Nicholas Dial

First Edition

Fulton Books
Meadville, PA

Published by Fulton Books 2025

ISBN 979-8-89221-713-2 (paperback)
ISBN 979-8-89427-331-0 (hardcover)
ISBN 979-8-89221-714-9 (digital)

Printed in the United States of America

Contents

Please visit insurancemakecents.com for additional resources.

You can also scan this QR Code to download a free worksheet.

To contact us, please send an email to:

hello@insurancemakescents.com

Inspiration behind This Book

It came out of nowhere. It was completely unexpected. A Monday night in December, my family went through a devastating medical event. My father-in-law was in rough shape, and my mother-in-law came to me asking for help. She was needing oversight on the insurance policies he had at that time. At nine o'clock that night, any insurance he had, he was stuck with. We could only hope that whatever he had would come through. Thankfully, it turned out to be amazing. Prior to that night, my mother-in-law stayed at home with their children. Since his medical mishap, she has yet to fill out a job application to supplement any income. She hasn't needed to. I'm glad to say that even to this day, they're doing very well.

Sometime later, I was sitting in Madison, Wisconsin, airport waiting for my plane. As I sat there, I found myself deep in thought. I reminisced over that incredibly stressful night that turned out so well. I felt humbled that I was able to step in and help my family in that capacity. It left me inspired. My inspiration turned to frustration when I began to think about another young man I met just a few months after my father-in-law's incident. Like him, so many people look at insurance with a great deal of skepticism and naiveite. This young man was about thirty years old. As I got to know him briefly, I learned that he had a wife and three kids. He was the only working as she stayed home to take care of their children. It was practically the same situation my own family was in.

I learned that he didn't have much in the way of insurance at all. As I began to suggest for him to consider certain types of insurance products, he developed a smirk on his face and, with a very arrogant tone, responded with, "Pssh, I don't need that. I don't plan on anything happening to me." I was stunned. Naturally, I can't make this guy do anything with insurance. I was simply hoping to offer him my help. But the arrogance baffled me. I felt so angry for his wife and his kids. I began to think of my own wife and children. To think what I would do to them if my arrogance got in the way of making wise adult decisions about finances is hard to comprehend.

As I'm waiting for my plane to arrive, I'm going from one thought of inspiration and relief to the thought of complete frustration. I began to feel a bit overwhelmed. To this day, I don't entirely know why it bothered me so much, but the only way I knew how to work through these thoughts was to begin writing them in a journal. I wrote about the interaction and contrasting realities between my father-in-law and this young man. I then continued writing about how I would suggest looking at insurance in a more pragmatic and strategic way.

After what seemed like an hour had passed, I realized that I had typed eight pages worth of a manifesto of "How to buy insurance and not wreck your family." Perhaps that title could've been catchier. It turns out that these are ideas that are missing in this industry. I don't blame nor think badly of that thirty-year-old. In his world, nothing devastating likely happened to him that would force him to think of insurance like my family and I did. What happened to my father-in-law is the inspiration for me to begin writing this material. Meeting that young man validated the information. My father-in-law is an incredibly smart man. I'm not sure how he managed to put his insurance together with such wisdom, but obviously, it worked so well for him and his family, while others are left in a perilous position, losing almost everything they own and cursing the insurance products they had as a scam. What I hope to bring here is a new way to look at insurance that hopefully would strengthen the structure of insurance on a more personal scale.

Disclaimer

The title is not meant to deceive anyone about how insurance can work or will perform for them. The title of this book and the subsequent information within are not meant to insinuate that insurance can make any money for anyone. This book will not offer any legal or tax recommendations, considerations, or opinions. It is best to consult with a tax or legal professional. It is also important to review each policy related to the individual insurance products for specific information, limitations, and exclusions. Each product may vary.

Glossary

Normally, the glossary would be at the end. However, to introduce you to the technical words now may help you understand the material that follows.

application. A form to apply for new insurance coverage.

beneficiary. A person or entity that is designated to receive any financial benefit from an insurance policy or other financial instrument.

co-pay. An initial payment made to a doctor or medical facility by the person insured on a health insurance policy.

deductible. A preestablished amount of money that an insured will pay before an insurance product begins to pay toward a claim.

disability insurance. An insurance product that pays out a monthly benefit upon becoming disabled through a doctor's diagnosis.

effective date. The time in which the insurance product begins to cover the insured.

health insurance. An insurance product that pays for a medical treatment on behalf of the person it insures.

insurance. A means of protection from financial loss in which, in exchange for a fee, a party agrees to compensate another party in the event of a certain loss, damage, or injury.

insurance policy. It is the structure of coverage in written form. It lists in detail what the policy will pay out and how to qualify for the monetary benefits it provides. Additionally, it will list limitations and exclusions that will limit or restrict the payout from the policy. (This material is very important to read and even have a qualified person [i.e., financial advisor, insurance consultant, or attorney] review as well.)

limitations/exclusions. A portion of the policy that lists the items that are limited or excluded from the policy coverages. As an example, preexisting conditions can be found here.

life insurance. Insurance that pays a beneficiary a sum of money upon the death of the insured.

maximum out of pocket. Total amount of money in a preestablished year that an insured will pay before health insurance pays most, if not all additional costs.

open enrollment. Time period during which you can make changes to or elect for new insurance coverage. One common place you'll hear this is through your employer.

premium. This is what is paid by the insured each month to have an insurance policy.

preexisting. A condition that exists prior to the insurance product being purchased and effective date.

Related to disability insurance:

elimination or waiting period. How long you wait before the benefit begins. Examples are 7 days, 30 days, and 180 days.

benefit period. How long you will receive the benefit. Examples are two years, five years, or until the "Normal Social Security Retirement Age."

benefit amount. The amount you receive in income from the policy. Examples are 60%, 66 2/3%, or 100%.

offsetting income. The disability policy considers other sources of income that you receive to determine your actual monthly benefit amount. This one can be confusing because it seems like you would get one benefit amount from your disability income on top of what you get from, say, Social Security Disability Income (SSDI), among many other sources. As an example, say you became disabled and you selected a $3,000 monthly disability benefit. After a review of your case, Social Security Disability Income says you'll receive $2,000 in monthly income. Offsetting income (according to the policy) will pay the difference of $1,000 to make whole the $3,000 monthly income benefit.

**Other industry-specific terms will be outlined within the material.

Acknowledgments

This project started as a rant on my iPad and became one of the most challenging and rewarding efforts of my career. Over the past five years, it evolved into a mission to help others make more informed financial decisions—especially around insurance.

To my wife, Erin—thank you. From day one, you supported this book's creation with relentless encouragement, selfless sacrifice, and a sharp editorial eye. Whether juggling kids, cleaning up the house, or reading dense sections out loud, you never let me quit. I truly couldn't have done this without you.

To my parents and in-laws—thank you for your lifelong support, your belief in me, and the love that's carried me through every season. To my siblings, my children, and extended family—you've shaped the person I am today. I'm proud and grateful to call you family.

To Tess Welch at Lunar Graphics—thank you for bringing this book to life visually and online. Your creativity and professionalism raised the bar.

Lastly, to the many friends, mentors, and supporters who stood by me through the highs and lows—thank you. The value you've added to mine and my family's life is immeasurable. I'll always be grateful.

Introduction

July 19, 1957—Ralph walks into a Ford dealership to look for a brand-new car. He meets with the salesman and finds a beautiful cherry-red Thunderbird. The salesman is talking up the car, offering for Ralph to sit in it, play with the AM radio, and even take it for a test-drive. Knowing he has looked at two other cars earlier (one selling for $3,500 and the other for $5,000), Ralph is curious if he could find a better deal here. He really likes the car, but he doesn't know a lot about it mechanically or technically. He is unable to tell which car is the better deal. The only information he can rely on is the price and what the salesman will tell him about it.

After about a thirty-minute test-drive and a conversation with the salesman, Ralph asks for the price. The salesman, while smacking his gum and standing proud in his pressed suit, says, "This car? I'll tell you what. It seems like you really want this car. I have three other serious buyers coming in this afternoon. But for you…I'll sell it to you for $10,000 out the door."

Ralph is stunned! "This one is even more than the first two I looked at! What is so great about this one?" he asked.

The salesman responds arrogantly, "You see, this is the only cherry red you'll find!"

Ralph simply offers his thanks and that he'll think about it. He walks out of the dealership perplexed at what he just heard. He's more confused now than he was when he walked into the first dealership. "Is the $3,500 car a lemon? Is the $10,000 car a rip-off? Am I sure that this cherry-red car is the ONLY one and it happens to be in my town?" His head is spinning. He goes home marinating in his confusion and frustration.

Fast forward to 1958—a senator from Oklahoma by the name of Mike Monroney proposed a bill called the Automobile Information Disclosures Act of 1958. In its nationwide adoption, it required each car dealership to fasten an invoice sticker (also known as a Monroney sticker) to each car being sold. It mandated the disclosure of equipment and pricing of any new automobile. It outlines the details of the car from the model and trim options to the actual price of the vehicle. In short, it made the fine print and cost of the car readable and understandable to the car-buying consumer.

Prior to 1958, this era was known for *Caveat Emptor*, Latin for "Buyer Beware." The consumer didn't have the resources or the ability to research different vehicles that we have today to determine if what they were buying was a good deal or not. Since the passing of this legislation, any prospective consumer has been armed with a wealth of knowledge and resources that have only evolved to help them in their vehicle purchases. By simply looking at the sticker, even the most novice car buyer in today's market could tell you a substantial amount more than the consumer from 1957. With the advancement in technology and resources that began with the Monroney sticker, this economic market has turned from Buyer Beware to *Caveat Venditor*, "Seller Beware."

Unfortunately, most of the services or products we can buy today do not come with Monroney stickers. One such product is insurance. Even the federal government has tried stepping in, in attempt to regulate the fairness of insurance. Unfortunately, it didn't accomplish all they were hoping for and consequently created lasting repercussions that continue to fall onto the consumer who purchases the insurance product to this day.

Insurance companies have spent a lot of money on advertising, with the help of cute animals or humorous catchphrases that are overly simplified and lack clarity of purpose. These advertisements are designed to make the consumer think that they need this policy. The bigger problem is the consumer would buy the policy for a specific reason, just to find out that it doesn't cover what they thought it would. One effect of these fancy slogans and simplified advertisements is that they make any friend, uncle, or random salesperson with an opinion the expert in insurance. The reality is that this can build a false sense of confidence in the consumer, leaving them with the financial repercussions of that purchase.

Therefore, how do you (the prospective buyer) know how or where to find the kind of coverage that would protect the bulk of your financial needs? Up until now, there have been very few resources and objective material that can help the average consumer better understand how they can be the expert in their insurance—until now! This book may not be a Monroney sticker for the insurance industry at large. However, what follows is an attempt to outline a practical strategy for selecting any insurance product. The goal is to strengthen your insurance acumen to help reduce or eliminate any wasted money spent on current and future insurance products.

The strategy

> When the blindfold comes off…does it even apply to you?

Every year, without fail, there are millions of people whose strategy of selecting insurance is no better than hanging their insurance options on a dartboard, blindfolding themselves, and then throwing the dart, hoping they hit the right one. When the blindfold comes off, they don't challenge what they hit (bought), but they embrace it. They protect it as if it's their saving grace for all their financial problems that may happen to them. Of course, it is never a planned event that would cause their personal economy to collapse. All too often, when a financial professional offers a different perspective, they (the consumer) will quote their uncle, cousin, boss, friend, or some form of advertising that told them that this is exactly what they should have! If their worst day were to ultimately happen, we would all be watching from the sideline along with their uncle, cousin, and friend as they go toe to toe with what life throws at them next.

"Statistically, three out of four people die from…," "Every two minutes, someone is diagnosed with…," "Just last year, (x)millions of people were involved in an accident," and so on. You've probably heard these statistics recently. Unfortunately, it doesn't answer the big question: Does it even apply to you? Just like having a monthly budget for your finances, having a strategy for insurance will only strengthen your finances, not stifle it. Insurance, by design, is meant to protect your money now, in addition to the money you will amass in the future. It should complement your investment plan or any other long-term financial goals you have (especially retirement). It's incredibly important to challenge the validity of any sales pitch or marketing that does not complement these two areas. No more throwing darts at the board. From this point moving forward, every policy has a purpose!

Another hurdle (and arguably the biggest) is finding someone to build your insurance plan. One common characteristic that your doctor, tax account, and financial advisor have in common is they often apply a diagnostic to prescriptive approach. When they see something wrong, they look to understand it and will diagnose a remedy to fix the issue. Insurance professionals (salesmen really) are often focused on a product-based selling approach. They have a product they'd like to sell and would suggest it based on you simply being in front of them. If you paint a picture well enough, anyone can imagine themselves on the canvas. The old-fashioned car salesman tries to help you envision yourself in the car, driving down the road with a huge smile on your face. Not far-off is the insurance professional who will use statistics and outdated marketing tactics to convey the message of your need to buy this one product. You can buy a lot of tangible products that are sold through the product-based selling approach, but insurance is far from a standard type of product.

Do not take this segment lightly! You might tell yourself, "I feel good. I look good. So I must be incredibly healthy." It obviously doesn't work that way. Unfortunately, we've all met someone who seemed to be the picture of what healthy looks like, only to get the diagnosis or worse. Just like your doctor can tell you how healthy you really are, financial professionals can help determine how healthy your finances are. But making the changes necessary to stay healthy is entirely up to you.

https://en.m.wikipedia.org/wiki/Monroney_sticker

Chapter 1

The Collapse of a Personal Economy

Andy was out with his wife, Rachel, doing some final Christmas shopping. As they were making their way to the checkout counter, Rachel thought Andy was messing around with her by trying to talk funny. Andy was trying all right, but it was not a joke as he was actually trying to talk. *Funny* would have been the preferred emotion that night. Instead, it was replaced with complete panic as Andy was having a stroke. What started out as a relaxing night turned traumatic in the hours that followed. Rushing to the ER, Rachel could only think about her husband and pray that they would get help in time.

In the thirty-three years of their marriage, Andy was the only one who worked in their family, while Rachel stayed at home raising their five children. Over those many years of working, there was no reason to think he would ever have a stroke. He visited his doctor every year. He had no medical markers that would've warned him of the potential of having a stroke. However, on that fateful night, a stroke did happen and would collapse their personal economy.

Andy had eight years left to work before he could retire. They had just over one year left on their mortgage and one last child to support through college. Like many people who plan toward retirement, they had plans to improve some things around the house. They were looking at opportunities to travel to visit their daughter, son-in-law, and grandkids who were out of state. Any hopeful thoughts of the rest of their lives together vanished that one night.

To say that was a nail-biting time those first couple of days would have been an understatement. The thought of Andy no longer being able to work was a dark reality for Rachel. As Andy lay in the ICU incapacitated, Rachel frequently traveled between the hospital and their home, praying the whole way that he would make a full recovery. As each day passed, she began to fall prey to the worry and dread of a horrible reality that became more and more evident—Andy may never work again.

When some of the dust settled from his initial treatment, it came time for Rachel to go over what kind of insurance Andy had prior to the stroke. As Rachel began sifting through the papers on the table, she would often say, "There must be something that can help here?" Page after page, the questions start sounding like, "Am I going to have to start selling stuff? Are we going to have to move out of our home we've been in for over twenty years? How are we going to afford to eat and pay for these new bills?" The questions seemed endless. Perplexed and incredibly weary, Rachel called me and asked if I would come over to help.

Within the hour, I was there sitting with her at the dining room table with the insurance papers she thumbed through earlier. Though she had an idea of what insurance was, she struggled to understand it and what to look for. We poured a cup of coffee, and I began to comb through the documents. Rachel sat quietly sipping on her coffee as I went through the policies he selected during the previous year's open enrollment. After a few minutes, I came across a *huge* gem. I looked at Rachel and quietly said, "I think I found what I was hoping for. I need the company to confirm, but if it's true, everything is going to be okay." Pointing at the page, I said, "We need to give this company a call first." As Rachel put the coffee cup down, her eyes changed from complete sorrow to a glimmer of hope. Andy's insurance selection was rebuilding their personal economy.

Fortunately, Andy had one of the best insurance portfolios set up prior to the stroke. Why was it so great? Because it actually worked for him after the stroke. Andy is a very intelligent man. He was meticulous about reading through everything before he bought any product. He also had an amazing insurance consultant within his company (and outside through his retirement advisor). Because of his insurance programs, Andy and Rachel didn't miss a normal bill after the stroke. They also paid off their house and put their last child through college, in addition to taking on more with the new medical bills. They did all this without Rachel needing to get a job. She was able to focus solely on Andy's recovery.

It goes without saying that there is nothing peaceful about Andy having a stroke. Rachel has a daily task to make sure her husband has everything he needs, in addition to making sure the bills are paid. Rachel often says how grateful she is that Andy set up his insurance programs the way he did. That in and of itself brings so much peace to the present day.

I sincerely hope that if you remember anything from this book, it would be this: Expenses without an income are called bankruptcy! Income with expenses is called peace of mind. There are plenty of insurance programs out there, and many we'll cover in this book. The illustration above is meant to prove how critically important it is to build an insurance strategy that will strengthen your finances and not stifle them.

Now, let's assume that the reason you're reading this book is that you know practically nothing about insurance and you do not currently have an insurance policy outside your car and health insurance. Additionally, you would like to build a strong insurance portfolio, and you have two requests:

1) "I want the best possible coverage," or "Cover my worst possible day."
2) "Don't waste my money."

That sounds a lot like "having your cake and eating it too," which is a figure of speech with a slightly negative connotation that suggests that you cannot have both. Within the insurance world, it's all about how you build it.

What follows is a road map for exploring the world of insurance and how to put an effective portfolio together. One point of caution to consider is that if you do the process out of order, you can create quite a financial problem for yourself. As you read through these next steps, if you already have enough money invested or saved to check off a particular insurance strategy, then simply move on to the next one. In some cases, you may check all the boxes with your own money. This is what the industry calls self-insured. For most, it seems utopian.

Unfortunately, many find themselves working all the way through retirement because they have a depleted retirement account. One may even argue that too much insurance could even be the single greatest drain on a quality investment strategy. If you're reading this and thinking that this might be you, then there is hope. The idea of self-insuring is not utopian. It can even be reachable. Hopefully, the coming pages will offer you a new way to balance your insurance enough to free your money up to invest and retire well. The idea is not to insure yourself for every possible thing out there. Rather, it's about having a proper balance between selecting insurance and investing your money that can help lead to the reality of being self-insured. Moreover, it will allow you to live a life without fear of the what-ifs. Dare I say, insurance might actually make sense!

Chapter 2

The Image

Insurance might actually make sense.

Income (The Castle)-Retirement/Investment/Savings (King/ Queen of the Castle)-Expense Management (The Mote around the castle)

We've all seen this image. There it stands, a strong, majestic, beautiful, fortified castle. Iron chains raise and lower the drawbridge over the mote that surrounds the castle. You then turn your gaze upward, above the columns and walls, toward the residence. From your view, you notice the tenants of the castle wearing their crowns clothed in their royal robes. As you take in this majestic structure, you begin pondering what it took to build such a fortress.

Though the image of the castle in general can take on different shapes and sizes, the strength of the castle is dependent on the material used to build it. If you tried to build your castle out of the water that belongs in the mote, then your castle will not stand very long. Building it with the proper stone and bricks is specific and intentional. You must also think about how tall you should build your fortress. Not building your walls high enough can cause anyone to get in without much effort. Also, any small army can start breaking down your walls if you don't have enough water in the mote. This is the leading image to take with you as you read along.

The structure

Here is the process. This has helped so many protect their finances without spending a lot of money.

- Income insurance (Castle)
    - Disability
    - Life insurance
- Retirement/Invest/Savings (You-King/Queen)
    - Self-insuring
    - Consistent building
- Expense management insurance (The Mote)
    - 99% of all insurance policies live here.

Chapter 3

Disability Insurance

The walls and columns

Imagine this: you're driving home from work, and as you're approaching an intersection, you ponder how nice a day it is and begin thinking about some of the yard work you can get done before...*bang*! Someone runs a red light. The scene is horrific, and they bring in a helicopter to fly you to the closest hospital. Moments after landing, you are rushed into emergency surgery. The chances of you surviving are slim. The doctor pulls your family aside and prepares them for the worst. Late into the night, your vitals improve. You start making slight movements with your fingers. After a couple of days of gradual improvements, the doctors adjust their prognosis. It appears that you're going to live. Your family breathes a huge sigh of relief until the next wave of stress comes. Two years is a long time to recover before you're released to go back to work.

The thought of becoming disabled is often the farthest thing from people's minds and for good reason. When was the last time you were ever disabled? Perhaps, a better question is, "When was the last time you didn't return to work after being sick or hurt?" Chances are, you would say, "Never." If we point back to the beginning of the book and Andy's illustration, it's not about whether we will ever become disabled, but it's if you were, how much money could you lose? For most people, that would be a lot of money! Losing an income can single-handedly demolish a personal economy.

All too often, people assume that disability is a catastrophic event like becoming paralyzed with a broken back or having an uncurable cancer. Though these are types of disabilities, they are not the definition of being disabled. Disability is a diagnosis from your doctor of a medical condition that restricts you from continuing your normal full-time employment. It could be for a shorter amount of time or for the rest of your career. For an insurance product, a disability policy is used to insure (protect) your income.

The way you can determine the amount of money you could lose by becoming disabled is to take your current salary and multiply it by your remaining working years (according to the current Social Security retirement age). What you will see is the income you'll need to insure (protect). As an example, let's take a thirty-year-old who makes $100,000 per year. Having 37 years left to work (retirement age being sixty-seven), he would make $3,700,000. The reality is, if he does not have over $3 million saved or invested, then the disability policy will be the most important insurance he will own throughout his career. There is quite literally no other insurance policy on the market today that will protect his income.

If you were to become disabled and use this program, the monthly dollar amount can vary based on the policy. The most common coverage is built around 60% of your normal salary. There are some considerations to keep in mind (i.e., taxes) that may affect your monthly income on this program. It is vital that you review any tax implications with a tax accountant. As a note, this book will not offer any legal or tax recommendations, considerations, or opinions. In addition, it is important to take the time to review your policy for exclusions and payout details.

Contrary to what we've thought...

At this point, you may have noticed that there's an extremely popular insurance that was not suggested, life insurance. Why do you think that is? Everyone with an idea of insurance agrees that you must have life insurance. But where should you put it in the priority list? For many, it seems obvious that it would be first on the list.

There is one issue slightly less challenging than using life insurance, and that's losing life insurance. If something happens where you survive, then the life insurance won't pay out its benefit. As a result, in addition to your mortgage, food, and utilities, you will have to add your life insurance premium to the growing list of expenses. Without an income, money will get tight quickly, and many of those expenses are on the chopping block to get rid of.

Arguably (for anyone who requires an income to function economically), disability insurance should be purchased before any other insurance product (including life, car, home, health, etc.). There's a good possibility that this idea has you shifting in your seat a little. This idea is contrary to what we've thought for years about insurance. It does not seem logical to buy another insurance product before life insurance because we all have a 100% chance of dying at some point. However, if the illness or accident doesn't kill you, then you may lose your life insurance entirely.

Soapbox alert! "A very bad habit…"

The main purpose of the disability product is to protect your income. That's it! Imagine over a thirty-year career, you've managed to show up not missing more than a couple of days of work for being sick or taking the yearly vacation. You may be like many who think "I don't plan on anything happening to me. I'll still show up to work." May I ask a pointed question?

Are we done being naïve about this? When was the last time you made anyone or anything do exactly what you want them to? Make the other car stop at the red light? Make the diagnosis just vanish? The purpose of this book is meant to challenge the way we've looked at insurance for decades. This book is built to offer a sense of realism in how we buy insurance as individuals. It's obvious that no one has been in a horrific car accident until that light turns red. No one is diagnosed with cancer until they walk into the doctor's office. No one has lost an income or a home until it's gone. Insurance by nature is meant to protect the unexpected or unplanned. It offers a glimpse into the future to know how the story ends (financially).

It was said earlier that as a society, we have a horrible habit of buying insurance like we buy cars and coffee. We buy them with the intention to use them. So when we buy insurance products solely on the probability of using the insurance product (especially disability), we make a grave mistake in proper financial planning. In the end, the people that are affected may not only be us but the family or individuals who rely on us financially. Insurance is not about if we will use it. Rather, it's about if we don't have this product, how much could we lose?

Soapbox over, moving on…

Disability
Image and application

It's a beautiful Monday morning, as you drive into work. As you come up to a red light you notice the construction project of some new commercial buildings. One building happens to catch your eye. It's not a building at all. It looks like a bunch of bars and platforms stacked on top of each other. This is typical of construction projects, particularly when cement or brick buildings are being built. Not long after the foundation and initial walls are built, they will construct a temporary structure called scaffolding, to help the workers build the walls higher and higher. As the building progresses from the ground up, the temporary structure stays in place until the building can sustain itself to finish the project without the scaffolding. That is the exact image of what disability (and life insurance) are within an insurance portfolio. They are the temporary structures (or scaffolding) to the building of your castle. When it comes time for you to either retire or your money has built a fortified structure of other investments around you, the temporary structure serves no additional purpose and is taken down.

There's an old proverb that says, "A rich man's wealth is his strong city." How that city is built is brick by brick. Over time, you will use your income to build your savings, retirement, and other investments that eventually work for you. During the time it takes for you to build your city, you can use insurance as a temporary structure to help build the walls.

The purpose of these two illustrations is to point out two key areas. Number one is you cannot build a tall and fortified structure if you can't reach high enough. You'll need the temporary structure for that purpose. The second illustration is the temporary structure also serves a secondary purpose for protecting the wall you're building. The aim here is to understand the right product to buy that serves as the best temporary structure.

From the ground up

One common problem so many run into is how to build the right insurance portfolio without spending too much money. If you spend all your money on insurance, you will likely struggle to pay your normal bills and grow any reasonable investments/retirement accounts. Contrary to a common myth in buying insurance, more money spent does not always mean better coverage. Cheaper doesn't always mean that the product is cheap. Disability and life insurance are designed to be very vanilla in their coverage. We will cover more on life insurance shortly. For disability, you are paying to protect your income. There's not a lot of sprinkles you need to add to it. With that in mind, how do you select the right disability policy to protect your income?

There are two main types of disability products sold: short-term and long-term disability. These policies are available for purchase on your own or potentially through your employer. Though these policies are designed to protect your income, they can look very different from each other. The strategy between them changes as well. These policies can come with a lot of details and fine print. What follows will help you in selecting your policy. Before we get there, let's go over the basic information first.

Short-term disability: it is exactly how it sounds

Short-term disability is a product that has a short elimination or waiting period, with a short benefit period. Following a disabling event, the monthly benefit can start as soon as the eighth day (if not immediately after the event) and last between six months to two years. Once the benefit period has been completed, the policy is done paying you a monthly benefit.

This policy has been quite popular for anticipated disabling events like pregnancy or planned surgeries. It's quite convenient to consider this as a paid-time-off or a sick-time option through your employer, especially if you don't have much saved. However, it can be a critical error to confuse this with a long-term disability policy.

Long-term disability: the single most significant insurance product

If you cut off a person's ability to create an income for the rest of their life, you limit them from being able to function economically. Their personal economy can and (likely) will collapse. For the vast majority of those who rely heavily on their income through employment, long-term disability is the most significant insurance program to select above anything else.

Finding a long-term disability product is not very hard. The most ideal place to look first would be through your employer. It will also be fairly easy to manage your policy there as well and could be cheaper. With this product (among others), there are some additional benefits of going through your employer, like expressed underwriting (not having to go through medical exams), and potentially some employer contributions (they help pay for it). Be sure to review the details with your human resources department. If you choose to select a policy outside your employer, keep in mind these policies can cost quite a bit more. It may also come with additional application requirements to determine your eligibility.

Long-term disability insurance may have some similar characteristics as short term with the elimination periods. Some programs can start paying a monthly benefit as early as a week (or earlier in some cases). Where it differs greatly from short-term disability is that it will pay you a monthly income until the age of sixty-five to sixty-seven (dependent on the policy), rather than ending after a couple of years (at the most). The trick to this policy is to pay as little money for it as possible while having a benefit that covers your lost income for the duration of your career.

Necessity vs. convenience

This segment will address the importance of rethinking how to buy disability insurance. All too often, people will buy the convenient policy first, which results in a lot of money spent. With long-term disability, you want to build it with your savings and sick time in mind. Here's an example to help illustrate.

It was in the middle of October, and Richard and Mike both received an email about open enrollment coming up. In the email, it encouraged all employees to review their long-term disability program. Hoping to glean some ideas on how to select the program, Richard asked Mike which elimination period he chose. Mike told him that he went with the ninety-day program. Richard went on the enrollment site and saw the difference between the thirty-day program and the ninety-day program. It was a few dollars cheaper, so Richard chose the ninety-day elimination period. Fast forward to February of that next year, Richard found out that he was going to have a surgery and that the recovery time was six months to a year. What he didn't know was Mike was also scheduled to have a surgery of his own with the same recovery period.

One year later, both men came back to work. Mike went up to Richard to see how his surgery went. Richard said the surgery was fine but the first few months were very difficult. After he exhausted his two weeks of paid time off, he had to fight with HR to understand why he couldn't continue to get paid. Due to his ninety-day waiting period on the policy, he had to break out a credit card just to make his bills for those two and a half months. After Richard finished venting on Mike, he asked how his time off went. Mike replied nonchalantly that it went well.

Richard asked, "How so?"

Mike responded, "During our open enrollment, I considered my savings and sick time to help build my disability program. We knew we had six months of savings, so we could afford those first three months. When I had my surgery, I used the two weeks paid time off and then spent our savings to pay our normal bills before the disability kicked in."

The strategy here is called overlapping. You can overlap your disability policy with your savings account (or other paid time off at your employer). Say you have three months of savings in the bank, and you select a disability program with a ninety-day elimination/waiting period. If something comes up that requires you to use part or all your savings' account, then that is where an income gap develops. What will happen is you will have to figure out how to create an income while you're unable to work. In this case, you might consider selecting a thirty-day elimination/waiting period instead in order to create the financial overlap. A second benefit of overlapping is, if you don't use your savings account prior to becoming disabled, you will have extra cash for any other expenses you'll need to pay for after becoming disabled.

If you buy the wrong one...

One error that many have made is the selection of the wrong disability program for their individual financial strategy. For many working people, to *only* buy short-term disability is a bad idea. Imagine it this way: Take a thirty-seven-year-old making $100,000 per year. Over the next thirty years, he would make over $3,000,000. If the policy pays the standard 60% of his salary over two years, he would receive $120,000, which means he would have left $2.8 million uninsured. If he was still disabled after those two years, his benefit would stop, and he would begin hurting financially. If he plans to work for the next thirty years, it would be wise to either buy a long-term disability program in addition to his short-term disability policy, which could cost him more each month in premium, or he could select a long-term disability product with a short elimination period (i.e., seven-day elimination/waiting period).

Many people have found value in the short-term disability program because it can be very helpful for planned periods of time off due to a surgery or the birth of a child. The error is their perception where they buy the short-term disability policy, thinking it will cover their income for the rest of their career, and it stops after those two years (or earlier).

Deeper dive

There are plenty of things that can complicate the selection of this policy. Having an insurance consultant who knows your strategy can play a vital role in positioning the right policy for you. At the risk of diving too deep here, I would suggest doing your research and asking questions about your disability policy to help educate yourself. Some questions you can start with are the following:

- How do I qualify for the policy?
- What are some exclusions that will keep me from receiving a benefit?

- How long will it pay out, and will the benefit amount change over time?
- Will the monthly benefit be offset by other sources of income?
- Once I receive a benefit, what are the tax requirements that I will be responsible for?

One key component of disability is tax liability. Are there taxes associated with receiving a benefit from your disability plan? *Before you're disabled*, it is highly recommended you connect with your tax accountant to determine if you'll be subject to taxes so you can have a plan in place, rather than being surprised. It would be helpful to review this section of this book, in addition to the rest of your policy with your insurance consultant for specifics about your current or prospective disability program.

A word of caution: Don't set and forget your insurance policies

One critical thing to note is that buying insurance is not a one-transaction event. Your strategy will change, and so should your insurance coverage. If you do not have a savings and, therefore, you're on the seven-day elimination period, you don't have to stay there. After a while, if you've managed to build a healthy savings account between three and six months, then you can (and probably should) adjust your elimination period. Likewise, if you're about to retire, long-term disability would probably be too expensive and may not serve much of a benefit to you. A case might be made for a short-term disability policy but only as a transition income into your retirement.

We'll get into the expense management programs a bit later, but this true story illustrates the importance of making sure you always keep your strategy of coverage in mind. This applies to income and expense management insurance policies alike.

During the late winter of 2022 in Boulder County Colorado, a random fire broke out. Unfortunately, Colorado is accustomed to fires, even within residential neighborhoods. What made this fire particularly devastating was how fast it went through this neighborhood. The wind accelerated the fire so much that homes were engulfed in less than an hour. Owners of these homes didn't even get a chance to pack anything. Important documents, family photos, and prized possessions were gone in a matter of minutes. The fire was put out, and the owners managed to survey what was left, which for many was nothing but ashes. Most of these homes were worth approximately $600,000. Unfortunately, it got worse. When it came time to get the insurance company involved, many owners found out that they hadn't reviewed their coverages in quite some time. When they opened their policy, their home was only insured for $400,000. This means the owners would have to come up with an additional $200,000 just to rebuild their home.

There are so many points to remember about buying insurance. This concept definitely lands at the top of the list. To only buy insurance once and never think about it again is a critical error. This concept is applied to any kind of insurance program.

Key points: Disability

- Disability is the primary insurance for your income.
- It is not about if you will become disabled, but it is how much you have to lose if you were to become disabled.
- Disability typically should be one (if not the first) insurance to establish before any other products, given the importance of the product.

Here is a list of specific terminology you can familiarize yourself with regarding the disability program. It helps to know them as you explore the disability program before you buy.

- Build your elimination/waiting period with your savings and sick time.
- Monthly benefit amount:
    - What percentage of income is it?
- Tax liabilities.

- Qualifications and exclusions for available coverage.
- Monthly premium.
- Short-term vs. long-term disability products:
    - How much of your income could you lose?

Chapter 4

Life Insurance

The walls and columns

Orlando was a polished insurance consultant. He built a strong reputation and client list within his community. People came from quite the distance to meet with Orlando.

Russ was a successful businessman in the same community as Orlando. He had heard from a friend that Orlando was the guy to meet with for life insurance, so he scheduled an appointment. Like so many others, Russ knew that having life insurance was one of life's many obligations. After doing some initial catch-up and "how's the family" conversation, Russ gets to the point and asks for a $500,000 life insurance policy. Not knowing who Orlando was, Russ expected the stereotypical sales presentation of the shiny features and benefits that Orlando was sure to deliver to get the sale. What happened next surprised him.

Orlando didn't reach for his computer to show the product. He didn't even reach for a pen and paper. Orlando simply sat forward in his chair and asked a thought-provoking question, "Russ, what are you trying to cover?"

Russ sat back as he pondered the question. He took a deep breath and said, "Well, I figure I would want it to pay off my house."

"How much is the house?" Orlando asked.

"$1.1 million," Russ replied.

Orlando thought about Russ's response with a curious look on his face. "So you have $600,000 in equity. May I ask a different question?" Orlando asked.

"Sure," Russ said, intrigued by Orlando's demeanor.

"Rather than passing away, you retire. Will you keep the house or look to downsize?" Orlando inquired.

"I would downsize. The house was more for the kids," Russ answered.

"If you pass away, would your wife downsize the home as well?" Orlando continued.

"Oh, she would definitely downsize!" Russ answered, now sharing Orlando's curiosity.

"Since you have $600,000 in equity, is it safe to say that you could simply sell the home and buy the next home with that equity?" Orlando questioned.

"Absolutely!" Russ answered.

Orlando paused for a moment to think and then asked, "Is there anything else you can think of that you might need this life insurance for, like replacing your income as an example?"

Russ sat back, took a big breath, and pondered. "Well, we have a sizable investment balance. The interest alone would replace my income without needing another job. So nothing else really comes to mind."

"That's really great, Russ," Orlando acknowledged. "It sounds like you've done a great job with your money this far, and it doesn't seem like you need to spend any more money on a life insurance policy when you already have your finances set up well."

Russ mused for a moment and replied, "Orlando, this was not the meeting I was expecting. I figured you would try to sell me the best life insurance product you have. Thank you for taking the time to explore this with me. I can see why you're so sought-after in this town."

Reality check

Arguably, life insurance is the one product that can single-handedly waste more money than nearly any other insurance product out there. The primary reason is how elusive it is. It is easy to understand as it pays out upon your death; however, the strategy of buying it seems to be a moving target. How much is enough, and when is too much, too much? Insurance salesmen, or even commercials, prey on the fear of not having enough life insurance. One common sales pitch in the industry today is, "(*insert random percentage here*) of people are underinsured when it comes to life insurance. Isn't it worth $20 more per month to make sure your family is covered?" The salesman would ask persistently. Marketing is designed to get you, as the costumer, to think about your need to buy the product and that a minimal cost should make it attractive to buy that product. Here's the problem: it's a vicious cycle that seems to only add more expenses to a monthly budget.

The reality of any life insurance policy is that it's the most selfish, selfless product you will ever buy. You buy it on yourself, for your death, to benefit someone (or something) else. The hardest part of this policy is at the point of buying this product, you must think through the moments that come immediately after your death and the financial impact it will have on your family, in hopes that they will be taken care of when you're gone. Many people buy life insurance policies just to find out they were wasting their money for the last ten, twenty, or even fifty years. This segment will bring a new view of legitimacy to the selection of life insurance. You will see some practical purposes of how to insure yourself properly all while minimizing any more wasted money spent.

Briefly, let's go back to the analogy of your castle for a moment. As you think about the towering walls and columns and vast amount of water that fills the mote, where do you feel that life insurance belongs? The best place for it would be alongside the disability insurance within the walls and columns as your primary defense against your most significant financial loss, which for many would be their income.

Unlike many insurance products that are built to help if a specific thing happens to you (i.e., cancer, car, cell phone, etc.), disability and life insurance are a bit more expansive in their coverage. It's not a matter of how you became disabled or how you passed away; it's the fact that you are disabled or you did pass away.

Before we get too far ahead, let's build this piece from the ground up. What is life insurance, and how do we look at it in a productive and strategic sense?

What is life insurance?

Life insurance is simple. For this benefit to be paid, it requires the death of the person it is ensuring. There are two types of life insurance products available: term and permanent. Term is typically set up in yearly increments (ten years, twenty years, thirty years), which is typically the lower-cost option. Permanent is built for seemingly the rest of your life and is normally the higher-cost product. Its maturity date is typically at or beyond age 100 respectively. Permanent life insurance is also known in the market as Whole Life or Universal Life.

In terms of strategy, you can think of term insurance to insure the thirty-year career, thirty-year mortgage, and the thirty-year dependent child (hopefully not). While you are working, you are amassing an income to pay off the mortgage, save for retirement, and raise the children to become financially independent. For many people, their largest need for this type of life insurance is during their working years, while their family relies so much on their income. If you pass away, your family would likely assume the difficult task of replacing your income. Term insurance allows for a (typically) lesser monthly premium in exchange for a larger sum of life insurance over the established timeline (ten years, twenty years, etc.).

Aside from very specific strategies that we won't cover here, the general strategy of permanent life insurance is for either final expenses (funeral, burial, lawyers, etc.) or other lingering expenses that would impact your family that may be present well after a term policy has expired. Because the policy is built to cover the duration of your life, the premium typically costs more per month than term insurance. These policies can get very complicated, and it's imperative that you work with your insurance consultant to review all the options and the fine print before selecting this product.

Term life insurance

If you don't have a substantial income or even a lot of equity built into your home, you probably could use a life insurance policy to help if you pass away. So how do you select a policy from the oceans of life insurance options? Simple, look at your money or the financial liability you'll leave behind.

Examples of financial liabilities are the following:

- Loss of income
- Larger debt payoff
    - Mortgage
    - Student loans
    - Shared debt
- Child(ren) expenses
    - Living expenses
    - College tuition

There certainly could be other business debts or financial responsibilities that someone else may be responsible for if you were to die unexpectedly. Here is a brief description of the main financial liabilities and how you could use a life insurance product to protect them.

Income replacement is set up the exact same way as the disability policy, with one exception. Instead of ensuring the rest of your career with a life insurance policy, you might consider insuring the next five to ten years of your income. If you bought a policy for the rest of your career (such as thirty-seven years), you will likely spend too much money on life insurance premiums. Let's take the thirty-year-old, making $100,000 per year. Ten years of his income would be $1,000,000. If he was making $50,000, then ten years of his income would be $500,000. Ten years of an income should be a reasonable number to help keep from obligating your family to replace your income immediately after your death.

Here is one critical point to consider. If your spouse is a stay-at-home parent to your children, consider buying life insurance for the same benefit for you both. Here's why. If you pass away, then your spouse would likely have to find a way to put your children in daycare and find a job that replaces your salary. For many, that could be quite challenging. But what if your spouse passes away? Then you might have to either quit your job or modify your employment to make sure you could afford the time to work and take care of your children.

Mortgage payoff is as it would suggest. If you own a house, you typically get a loan to buy that house called a mortgage. Common mortgages are typically a fifteen-year or thirty-year mortgage. Naturally, the house can grow its monetary value larger than the balance of the mortgage, also known as equity. Over that same period of time, while the equity is being built, there is a chance that you could pass away. That's exactly where term life insurance can help. This type of life insurance can help with paying off the balance of the mortgage after your passing. As an example, let's say that you're married with two kids. Chances are, without life insurance, your spouse would need to take over the monthly mortgage payments. In short, having life insurance to pay off the balance of the mortgage can immediately take the financial pressure off your family.

However, if you were like Russ in the earlier example and the equity in your current home would cover the purchase of a different house, then this life insurance may not be needed.

Children are a significant thought when it comes to life insurance. The general illustrative verbiage for having life insurance for your children is paying for college. Paying for college is a euphemism for having expenses that come with raising a child. Selecting the most appropriate term policy is relatively easy to calculate. If you take your youngest child and add ten, twenty, or thirty years (hopefully not thirty years), how old would they be? Based on the answer, would they still be financially dependent on you? The most common policy in this case would be a twenty-year term.

One minor detail has left several confused. If they are buying life insurance to replace an income, pay off their mortgage, and help financially raise the remaining children at home, all three do not require their own life insurance policies. For many, having a larger life insurance policy (calculated within the income category) should suffice for many as enough coverage. The primary objective here is to accurately account for each one and bring them together within one policy. To use the thirty-seven-year-old example again, if he were trying to protect eight years of his income ($800,000) and pay off the last $200,000 of his mortgage, then having a $1,000,000 life insurance policy should be enough.

Permanent life insurance

Briefly, let's review the characteristics of permanent life insurance. It is typically a long-term policy, usually maturing (ending) around age one hundred if not longer. Because of this fact, the premiums can be considerably higher each month than term insurance. The strategy for this program is significantly different as we'll go over shortly. One critical thing to note is if you try to insure any of the financial liabilities from the term life insurance programs here, it can become very costly to have this product. It's highly recommended that you review your strategy with a financial advisor and/or insurance consultant before buying any life insurance product. Below is the common area for which you would select a permanent life insurance policy.

Final expenses

Burial, funeral, lawyers, taxes—all these are examples of final expenses. When someone passes away, the costs associated with the burial and funeral would be coming out of your family's or friends' pockets. When it comes to dividing your estate, having legal counsel to properly execute your estate will also add an additional expense. Death taxes should be considered as well. It would be helpful to consult with an attorney and tax professional to better plan for your estate transfer and taxes that would be relevant after death.

Errors with buying life insurance

Several common and recurring errors are made when buying life insurance. The industry has not helped with solving these problems with its continual marketing campaigns and outdated sales tactics. Here are just a few known errors with buying life insurance.

How much is too much?

Life insurance can be found practically anywhere, from your retail store to the independent sales contractor. Moreover, these companies are often not taking the time to explore what life insurance you may already have. They are looking for the next sale. One common question that is asked is, "Are you sure you have enough?" This is where you must know how much insurance you need, how much you have, and where the life insurance is located (to include your employer). Knowing all this will help keep you from over-insuring yourself.

Once you've attained the proper amount of coverage, you should go into maintenance mode. Be sure to check your individual financial strategy regularly to ensure that the amount of coverage is indeed enough. Also, make sure to stay connected with the company that holds your policy for any premium and benefit changes. Term life insurance will usually adjust their premiums following the ten-, twenty-, or thirty-year period. At that point, review your present financial strategy, and if you need to extend the policy, you can explore the options at that time. If your financial strategy changes where it requires more life insurance, then know the number you need to insure and maintain the policy as well.

"Worth more dead than alive..."

One incredibly concerning phrase is, "I am worth more dead than alive." Having too much life insurance is not a noble cause. The one that it hurts the most is you. It may seem obvious, but when you die, you don't receive that amount of money. It seems as if those who have a large death benefit buy it as if they will win the lottery when they die. Unfortunately, buying too much life insurance happens way too often, and in the end, the retirement account or even the personal savings account is the area that suffers the most. It is imperative to know the actual number you need to insure.

Employer's life insurance

This is a hidden gem and underutilized within a life insurance strategy. Life insurance through your employer can cost very little each month if nothing at all. These policies range from as small as $10,000 up to several times your salary. Though it can be very helpful to the employee, there is often one primary misperception about this program, and that is known as portability or your ability to take it with you when you leave. In most cases, you cannot take the policy with you when you leave the employer. If you can take it with you, (typically) it's a convertible policy and will increase its premium dramatically. In some cases, the benefit also decreases as you get older.

If you can increase your life insurance through your employer, this would be a great strategy to cover more of your income without spending a lot more money. Typically, you'll see this listed as 5x salary (as an example). This means if you make $100,000 per year, then you can have $500,000 in coverage. Again, this amount is usually while you're employed at your current job and likely won't be available to go with you if you were to leave.

Life insurance for children

We've made it this far in the insurance conversation but now seems that we've entered the area of taboo. We can talk all we want about our own misfortune and how we can insure that; however, when a child is involved, now, it gets uncomfortable. As a father of three, I would relate that it is never an easy thought, let alone a conversation to have. The only way I've found to have this conversation is direct to the point and don't stay long.

If a child passes away, the simple reality is the financial burden is left to the parents/family of that child. One day, I managed to speak briefly with a lady about this very subject. Unfortunately, she had lost a son in a car accident. Interestingly enough, she had bought a life insurance policy for her son just one year prior. She mentioned how, without the policy, she would've had to pay for those expenses with a credit card and be reminded of his death every time she would go to pay the credit card bill. Life insurance allowed her to separate herself financially from that horrific day.

The reality of life insurance is it is meant as a strategy and not solely as a product to purchase. So here is a brief and simple point for life insurance for children.

A) *You don't need a lot.* You're not trying to protect their income because they likely don't have an income that you rely on. They don't have a mortgage because they live with you. Your child relies on you, not the other way around. When it comes to selecting a child's life insurance, the purpose listed above covers the expenses of any funeral, burial, or additional expenses that come with death. That's the basic idea.

B) *Keep their long life in mind.* Death isn't the only thing to consider. If a medical condition occurs (i.e., diabetes, cancer, among others), it could limit their ability to select an insurance policy later in life. By having a life insurance product prior to a diagnosis, this could allow them to continue some level of coverage throughout the rest of their life. Lastly, be cautious that the policy you select is stable in premium and benefit, meaning that neither will change throughout the life of the policy.

To close out this section, here is a final thought. Life insurance is a critical piece of strategy to employ. It stands right next to disability, fortifying the walls of your financial castle. It is also one of the easiest ways to lose money as well. All too often, it is said that "you may never have enough." That statement alone is relative.

How much is enough, and is enough, enough? The reality is, like any product, you may pay too much for something you don't even need. In contrast, you may not pay a lot for just the right product. It takes wisdom and a little education to establish yourself in this area. The simplicity of just doing math offers the validation and confidence of the life insurance you select (or any insurance product for that matter). On our website, you'll find a worksheet that you can plug the numbers in for yourself to see exactly how much insurance you need based on a mathematical strategy.

Key points: Life insurance

- Two primary product types, term and permanent.
  - Term has the same strategy as the disability insurance produce.
    - Income replacement
    - Mortgage payoff (or other larger debts)
    - Raising children
  - Permanent is built for longevity and for final expenses.
- Know the amount you need to insure. The math is very similar to the disability section with replacing an income.
- Over insuring will result in spending too much money on the product.

Chapter 5

Retirement/Investments/ Savings

The residence of the castle

Imagine for a moment, you're in your castle, looking out of your living room window across your courtyard. It is beautiful, decorated with flowers and fountains. You notice the towering walls and columns that stand tall with the finest stone found in your land. As you take in the view, you can't help but feel a sense of gratitude. This is the effort you put into your work and career. Let us go back to the proverb, "A man's wealth is his fortress." This is what you protect and now can enjoy for the rest of your life, the legacy you can leave to your family, the wisdom and tangible value that they will assume and carry on after you.

Here is a small disclaimer. This book is not about nor offers any investment advice. The material is meant to highlight the importance of investing and estate planning. For specific investment advice, it is highly encouraged that you contact a licensed financial advisor. It bears to say that this step is the epicenter of most financial goals. This is the purpose of having insurance: so that you can have your hard-earned dollars work for you and live on after. Though we may not go too deep into the details here, please do not overlook the importance of this segment.

Income-retirement-expense management

If you're like most who spend the bulk of your adult life working, you probably dream of the day to have the ceremony, get the watch, and make your way to the golf course, lake, or anywhere else that is no longer the stereotypical nine-to-five job. Throughout your career, what is the best way to organize your insurance to not take too much away from your investments but also build a strong strategy of insurance products? There are three simple steps: income, retirement, and expense management. The first two insurance products (disability and life insurance) are meant to protect your income. If you're disabled and are using your disability policy, then hopefully, you have managed to establish your income enough to keep your retirement account intact. If you pass away? Then your retirement and savings account are indeed the monetary gift that is left to your family and friends.

Expense management described in the next segment can help you from being obligated to withdraw from your retirement or other savings accounts prematurely. It's the mote around your castle. The material within the expense management portion is not well presented within the industry as they are sold as individual commodities. In short, having a better understanding and practical knowledge will ultimately protect the heart of your finances right here in your retirement planning.

Please keep this in mind. Even a good insurance policy can stifle any great investment opportunity. If it's a bad policy, well, what more needs to be said? Overspending on insurance or selecting the wrong policies can dramatically affect your finances. The peace of mind given to you by a well-executed insurance plan should help you live well during your later years. Your insurance policies should complement your investments and not stifle them.

Insurance is for the protection of the money that you do not have yet. If you continue to buy insurance policies for nearly everything, you likely won't have the money for your retirement. Insurance premium is money spent; you won't get it back unless you use the policy. To put it plainly, paying for insurance is a waste of money. The goal here is to learn how to waste money well.

Chapter 6

Expense Management

The Mote

How did a toothpaste company significantly change how we purchase nearly everything? Several decades ago, this toothpaste company needed a way to boost their profits. They challenged their staff to increase their sales without giving any additional marketing dollars to gain those sales. What they ended up doing was nothing short of genius. The result of their marketing seemed like an overnight success. They simply modified their commercials already running on TV to show the application of placing the toothpaste on their entire toothbrush. You might be thinking, *You're supposed to have toothpaste from one end of the brush to the other... right?* It turns out that they ran that commercial for all these years and made an amazing profit because of the over-usage of toothpaste. The consumer went through the tube faster and ultimately needed to buy more toothpaste sooner. *Eureka*! The company is now significantly more profitable. The moral of the story is that if a company can make you think that something always goes a certain way, you're conditioned to think that way without challenging it. Insurance has become one of the most notorious beneficiaries of this ploy.

Arguably, expense management insurance products make up nearly 99% of all insurance products out there: car, home, health, cell phone, dog, blender, on and on and on. There is insurance for seemingly everything. If you're traveling and miss your flight, there's insurance for that. If something breaks two years after you brought it home, don't worry; take it back for a warranty replacement.

As it was stated earlier, expense management insurance products is the mote around your castle. The concept of a mote was to keep any intruder from having easy access to your castle or finances in this case. Income insurance provides the pipeline of income to you and your family, where expense management is designed to help keep you from spending too much money. Take car insurance as an example. If you were in a car accident and it was your fault, by having car insurance, you are not having to pay for your car, their car, or the medical bills. After you've paid your deductible, your car insurance will replace the cars for you, same thing for a house. If it burns to the ground, you'll pay your deductible, and the insurance company will write the check to rebuild it. Rather than you having to pay for the car or the home, your insurance policy does that instead.

However, if you find yourself spending money on an array of insurance products, there may be very little money left over to grow your investment and retirement accounts well. The material that lies ahead will help illustrate how expense management policies look and work. The goal here is not to keep you from buying any insurance product at all. In fact, like disability and life insurance, it will help underline the purpose of these programs and how to build a strong mote around your financial castle.

https://openwebsolutions.in/blog/myth-fact-story-renowned-toothpaste-company/

https://www.armandhammer.com/en/articles/how-much-toothpaste-to-use#:~:text=Dentists%20recommend%20using%20a%20pea,erupts%20until%20age%203%20years.

Chapter 7

Examples of Expense Management Insurance Products

- Health insurance
- Car insurance
- Homeowners insurance
- Renters insurance
- Umbrella policies
- Supplemental coverages (accident, cancer, hospital, etc.)
- Extended warranties
- Liability insurance
- Enhancements to existing policies (e.g., adding on to disability insurance)

Obviously, there are a lot of expense management policies out there. It would take many more pages just to explore them all. Perhaps in future material, we can unpack these policies one at a time. For now, the purpose of this book is to offer two primary points: one is to help you understand the vernacular behind insurance in general, and number two is to expose the pitfalls related to these types of products that are so common. These types of insurance policies cover at least 99% of all available insurance options out there and can be bought through seemingly anyone or anywhere. In the end, even the most insignificant amount of premium can add up against your own savings and investment strategy if purchased poorly.

Chapter 8

Structure of Expense Management Policies

When it comes to any expense management policy, the vernacular can become a bit confusing. Scheduled benefits, deductible, co-pay, co-insurance, maximum out of pocket, and premium, among many others—what do they all mean? We'll briefly go through the idea of these points, and hopefully, this will illuminate any coverage you consider in the future. Here's a hint: most insurance policies follow this linear frame of coverage and vernacular.

Many expense management policies are built on a scheduled benefit. Scheduled benefit means that it has a preestablished list (schedule) of what the insurance product will pay for. As an example, health insurance will list the various areas of coverage and how much it will pay. Areas like primary care physician (PCP), specialist, emergency room, and prescriptions, among many others, will be listed here along with their respective coverage amounts.

For car insurance, the policy will list how much the insurance will cover for things like glass repair, comprehensive, and collision amounts. Most insurance products attach what is called a benefit summary page to their policies. This is where you can find most of this information.

Many expense management insurance products require some form of cost-sharing between you and the insurance. You will pay a portion, and the insurance will pay a separate portion.

Your portion

Co-pays, deductibles, co-insurance, and maximum out-of-pocket expenses, all, indicate your financial obligation to pay in conjunction with the insurance portion. One of the most known out-of-pocket obligations is called the deductible.

A *deductible* is your immediate out-of-pocket cost before the insurance company will pay anything. Though the definition is relatively the same, how it is applied can vary based on the specific insurance, which can make it somewhat confusing to understand in general. In health insurance, you'll have to reach your deductible before they'll begin covering any other bills. A separate way a deductible is applied is if you were in a car accident and need your car repaired. The insurance company would calculate the total cost of the damage and write a check for the repairs minus your deductible. The deductible amount is what you would pay directly to the shop.

When it comes to your insurance coverage, casually speaking, *co-pays* are a way of paying to play. You would usually see this when using your health insurance at a doctor's office or an emergency room. The concept is that if you want to be seen, you pay this predetermined amount (i.e., $25 co-pay for doctor, $500 deductible for the emergency room). Depending on your health insurance policy, there may be additional treatment or diagnostic procedures that would be billed beyond your co-pay. That is where your deductible would be brought into the billing process. Normally, you will pay your co-pay at the office and then receive a bill from the provider. This will be in addition to an explanation of benefits page from your health insurance indicating your portion to pay. The explanation of benefits can validate the bill you just received from the doctor or emergency room. If you already paid your full deductible for the year, then your out-of-pocket costs go to a co-insurance benefit.

Co-insurance is when the insurance policy begins paying for some of the costs of your medical bills. Typically, this particular benefit is found within your health insurance. If you were to look at your benefit summary page on your health insurance, you'll see the co-insurance listed (i.e., 80%/20%). This means you will pay 20% of any bill, and the insurance company pays 80% until you've reached your maximum out of pocket. It's important to add that you need to reference your policy for exact co-insurance payouts and how they apply to the established network within your policy.

The term *maximum out-of-pocket* can be quite confusing at first. Often, many believe that they have to pay both dollar amounts listed at the deductible and maximum out of pocket. This is not correct. Your maximum out of pocket is made up of your co-pays, deductible, and co-insurance combined. This is the total amount you would pay each year.

Here is one way this could look. Let's say you have a $2,000 deductible, with an 80/20 co-insurance, totaling a $4,000 maximum out of pocket. Once you've satisfied your $2,000 deductible, then your co-insurance comes in saying you pay 20% of any bill up to the remaining $2,000. This would equal a total of $4,000 as a maximum out of pocket.

When it comes to health insurance specifically, there are two serious pieces you need to know about the insurance program: in-network versus out-of-network, in addition to limitations/exclusions. Out-of-network is outlined where the insurance product will *not* cover or will limit their coverage. If the treatment is in-network, then the insurance company will often honor the coverage benefit that is outlined in your policy. Exclusions are what the insurance company has established that they won't cover, even if it is in network. These are often listed within the policy itself. It is highly encouraged you read through them before selecting the policy.

As a point of reference, limitations and exclusions are often attached to any kind of insurance policy, not just health insurance.

This segment uses health insurance as the primary example mainly because it encompasses all these pieces in one program. However, this segment can easily be applied to nearly any insurance product out there. Your individual insurance plan will go over the distinctions and specifics of their scheduled benefits. It also varies between different types of insurance (i.e., car, homeowners, dental, etc.). It's very important to read through each policy you receive to understand exactly what the benefits are and how much you must pay if you use it.

Unlike disability and life insurance, these types of policies can fluctuate throughout your life, if not changed every couple of years. One area that can change is your own personal finances. Eventually, you may be able to consider other self-insurance options, where you might afford a higher deductible, or forego the insurance together. In other instances, a specific scenario may implore you to consider buying the added coverage or lowering your deductible. Because of the fluctuations in your own personal economy, expense management policies are most certainly not a "set it and forget it" type of program.

Key point: Structure of expense management

- Many insurance products follow the same shared-costs model (i.e., deductible).

Chapter 9

Plan for Your Insurance

Because none of the companies have sponsored this material, I won't begin to give any credit. You've probably seen it on TV. You know what it looks and sounds like. You can think of the jingle, the slogan, the animal, or the humorous catchphrase. All the money spent on marketing is meant to remind you of how much you need their insurance products.

Aside from the federal government mandating certain types of insurance (i.e., car and health), no one else offers a sense of proper planning for selecting insurance products. Once they play on the heartstrings enough, human nature will kick in. The minute someone is diagnosed with (name it), their immediate community will often look at what coverage they don't have (regardless of whether they need it or not) and eventually buy the product.

Here is the thesis of this short but very important segment. What was stated earlier proves how important it is to know what you're exposed to losing financially if something happens to you. This is why you might buy that specific insurance product to protect against your financial loss. Just as important is also knowing the amount the insurance product will cost you per month and how much the insurance program will cover you during an event. All this should be considered before buying the policy.

From health insurance to extended warranties, all these costs add up over the course of the month only to drag your available budgetary dollars down. One might argue that as a society, we look to insure our bad days away, regardless of how much it may cost us.

Ironically enough, the amount of money we spend to keep the bad days away ultimately creates bad days when we've spent too much money.

The reality of insurance is simple. Insurance without a plan is practically wasted money. It wouldn't be an exaggeration to say that most people cannot recite the purpose of their insurance policies on a basic level. Like the old proverb says, "Who would start to build a home before first counting the cost, lest they start and can't finish, and everyone laughs at them." Obviously, no one will be laughing at you for whatever insurance products you select, except maybe yourself after wasting that much money. One thing that a toothpaste company did is ingrain into our society that over-usage is a good thing, where in fact it adds no more practical value. Insurance is often the same way. As it was said earlier, like any consumable product, we spend money to use it. We inevitably do the same thing with insurance, which can thus waste our money. The art is not to avoid wasting money entirely on insurance but rather to waste money well on a good insurance selection strategy.

Key point: Plan for your insurance

- Know what you are exposed to losing financially (practically) and insure that situation. To buy every insurance product offered can easily waste your money unnecessarily.

Chapter 10

Understanding the Coverage

Example: health insurance

Lacy just received an email from her employer letting her know that open enrollment started this week and they needed to make their insurance selections before Friday. Like the rest of her coworkers, she opened the email link to the enrollment site. Once inside the enrollment link, she finds the health insurance tab, with three links titled Low, Mid, and High plans for health insurance. Lacy thought to herself, *I'm healthy. I go to the doctor for my yearly checkup, but other than that, I only have the occasional accident.* She clicks on the low plan, and the deductible is $5,000 for the year. Her eyebrows raise, and a slight breath leaves her mouth. She thinks to herself, *Wow! That's a lot to pay before the insurance will kick in.* She scrolls down to the premium portion. It reads, "$277 per month." Lacy lets out a more audible gasp. "That's expensive," she muddles to herself. Lacy then clicks on the middle plan, thinking, *This one is probably more, but maybe the coverage is better?* As the page loads, it reveals a $3,000 yearly deductible. She scrolls down to the premium, and it reads, "$433 per month." Rather than gasping, now, she's shaking her head. "How does this make sense?" She ponders both plans and starts to think, *Well at least I won't pay as much out of pocket.* As she starts to move the mouse to enroll in the mid plan, there's an unsettling feeling. Lacy feels like she is back to one of her final exams, and the answer she's about to select is seemingly wrong, but she can't remember why.

Put yourself in Lacy's shoes. Why do you think selecting the mid plan might be wrong for her?

The answer is revealed by doing math within the insurance product. The difference between the low plan ($277) and the mid plan ($433) is $166 in premium per month, which equals $2,000 more spent in premium every year. She would spend that money just to potentially save $2,000 in her deductible by selecting the mid plan. There are no savings at all. That is a lot of money to spend for only going to the doctor's office once per year and having the occasional accident. Lacy would guarantee herself to spend the $2,000, while not receiving the $2,000 in savings if she doesn't use her health insurance much that year.

There is one caveat to mention. If Lacy was dealing with a medical condition that would result in her spending her entire maximum out of pocket before the year is over, then having a lesser deductible (greater premium) might make sense. One very important practice to get into is understanding how much money you'll spend over the course of a month, year, or however much time you'll have the insurance policy versus how much coverage you'll receive. The worksheet on our website will allow you to apply this math to your health insurance to show you how much you could be spending in a given year.

This is obviously the health insurance example. However, you can apply this to nearly any insurance policy out there. Sometimes, buying up on the car insurance or homeowners insurance isn't always meant to save you money. Doing the math to equate how much you'll spend in the monthly premium versus how much you'll spend out of pocket before the insurance begins to pay is an important number to know before buying the next insurance product.

Though insurance is meant to cover the unexpected, some things in life can be somewhat predictable and allow you to plan your insurance accordingly. It may validate the need to pay a little more each month for more coverage during a certain time. Take the homeowners insurance example from earlier. Real estate prices and insurance policies may fluctuate predicably because of economic cycles. One important piece to remember is that as the value of your home increases, your homeowners insurance policy will not automatically adjust, thus the significant financial impact it had on those homeowners who lost their homes that day of the fire. Nearly all insurance policies act that way as well. This underscores the importance of not forgetting about your insurance policy after you purchase it. Making a point to sit down with your insurance consultant regularly (like you would with your doctor) to go over potential coverage changes will keep you in front of any devasting issues where your insurance would play a vital role.

Key points: Understand the coverage

- Having a cheaper deductible and more expensive premium does not mean you're actually saving money. Calculate the premium vs. maximum out of pocket to help determine the total amount you'll spend.
- You can also apply this to other insurance products, not just health insurance.

Chapter 11

Start Building

The purpose behind this book is simple. The primary goal here is to help restore clarity to you as the consumer and confidence in whatever insurance you have and the insurance products you may consider. All insurance will do is to help you financially with the big what-if. The point to remember here is you can cover all the what-ifs that you please, but how much money will you have left after you've paid for all the premiums? Have you spent so much on insurance that you have to say goodbye to the new house, car, vacation, or even the nice retirement? Insurance is not the ultimate saving grace. Instead, it is possible for you to build your castle so well that in time, your money may offer a self-insurance plan turning most insurance products obsolete. As you've read a few times already, buying insurance is not about the vast amount of products you can buy. Rather, it is about establishing a sound insurance strategy that helps you with the what-ifs that you're exposed to, which can affect you financially.

First stone on the wall

At this point, you may have a better perspective on insurance at large and how to apply it going forward. There is still one more hurdle you may feel you have to jump. Where do you look, and who do you talk to, to find these products? How do you get from Point A (right now) to Point B (where you want to be), which offers you peace of mind, knowing that you have a stronger insurance structure for your future? There are three checkpoints between Points A and B: your employer, your financial advisor, and your insurance consultant.

Your employer

For many, the first stop for buying insurance will begin at their employer. There are two excellent reasons to go through your employer.

1. Lower premiums
2. Not having to jump through many hoops to get insurance

They can really offer a suite of available benefits that you can opt into for yourself and your family. One advantage of going through your employer is their application process. Usually, when you select specified insurance like disability or life insurance outside your employer, it requires you to go through a medical exam. In some cases, your employer might have what is called a simplified issue or expressed underwriting, which means it may not require any exams and just a few medical questions.

One important thing to do here is reach out to the human resources department so they can help you better understand how their current insurance programs are set up and how they might change in the future so you're not caught off guard. Here are a couple of points to keep in mind with your employer's insurance:

1. Premium/coverage changes. Though there are some advantages with lower-cost premiums through your employer, those premiums can change from year to year. In addition, sometimes, the coverage may change as well. It's best to keep this in mind, as many find themselves caught off guard, believing that their insurance through their employer is meant to stay the same, forever.
2. Portability. "Take insurance with you." Some (if not all) insurance programs available through your employer are not portable, meaning you won't be able to take them

with you when you leave your job. Life insurance is one of the most common that can leave many confused, thinking they have coverage when in fact they don't. You will want to review each program individually to determine this very characteristic. If you are able to take it with you, be aware that the monthly premium and/or the benefit could change.

With any selection of insurance at your employer, it's a good idea to review it with your financial advisor and your insurance consultant. If your employer doesn't offer the benefits you're looking for, the next place to look is your financial advisor.

Your financial advisor

Your financial advisor will know your long-term financial goals and what you're looking to accomplish. They will give you a reasonable assessment of the "health" of your financial portfolio. Medical physicians often prescribe medications (products) to improve and protect your physical health. Similarly, your financial advisor can have products they could prescribe that would improve or protect your financial health. A mark of a high-quality financial advisor is that they first look to understand your financial goals and the current state of your finances. After having a reasonable understanding of your information, they will build the blueprint of what your finances will look like with reasonable accuracy. From there, they can teach you about the structure of the insurance products. It's not that they won't sell you anything. On the contrary, they should offer the most appropriate product that compliments your financial future.

Here is one word of caution though. Financial advisors and insurance consultants who are worth their weight will carry the responsibility of managing your investment and/or financial portfolio with integrity. Just like insurance agents, there are some financial planners who offer some amazing products and others who offer awful ones. It is a bit ironic and unfortunate when a financial advisor would sell a bad product, rather than protect and your finances.

Their name suggests that they advise your finances. Remember this, you don't need to be the expert in *all* investments or insurance. You just need to be the expert in yours! When you know the math behind your insurance (premiums, coverage, etc.), you're much more capable of telling when you're being sold a bad product versus when that product is actually a good idea.

Unlike employer insurance, the products that financial advisors and insurance consultants have may come with applications that have underwriting requirements. This is where you have several questions to answer in addition to going through some sort of medical exam. In some cases, the underwriting can be quite extensive. Be prepared to see larger premiums than at your employer. Make sure these policies fit within your monthly budget and that you understand how they apply to your financial structure. If there isn't a particular policy that your financial advisor can offer, then the last step is your insurance consultant.

Insurance consultant

Very similar to financial advisors, insurance consultants will look to understand you and what you're hoping to accomplish financially. They will first look to understand your current insurance programs in place. Based on your financial goals, they will assess how your current insurance products are working to attain them. Based on the initial evaluation, they may recommend a product that could be missing or that may help strengthen your insurance strategy. Keep in mind that as they look through what you currently have, if you've potentially selected a product in error, they will likely suggest replacing it. Keep your thinking hat on for this, as they will explain why and how they would go about transitioning into a more appropriate product. This area has often been used prematurely by the standard salesman of insurance products. You want to be in alignment with your understanding of not only the product they are suggesting but also how it applies to your financial goals. If you find yourself confused after their suggestion, consider going back to your financial advisor for a second opinion.

Insurance can make sense!

You as the insured don't have to become an expert in insurance. You only need to be the expert in your insurance strategy and what you need or don't need! This system has worked time and time again. It has saved so much money for many people by revealing the fine print and purpose of the products. Hopefully, this book accomplishes something like the Monroney sticker did, which is to help you (the consumer) know a lot more about what insurance is and how it can be used. One goal of this book is to help even the playing field of understanding regarding any marketed or sold insurance product out there. Dare I say it, insurance can make sense!

Final Thoughts

When it comes to TV commercials, insurance companies place the start of their fine print on the bottom of the screen. One phrase that is missing is similar to a prescription drug commercial: "Not right for everyone; consult your financial advisor to determine if this product is right for you."

In writing this book, I've thought a lot about how I hope this book brings clarity to *you*, the reader, who makes the conscious decision to want to learn more about a moving target that is insurance. The industry is loaded with hundreds, if not thousands, of companies vying for your business. It's a tough market for the consumer, just like buying a car in 1957. When the Monroney sticker finally came out, it brought so much more clarity to the car-buying experience. Each insurance company is fighting to set itself apart in our current economic market. They will use countless marketing campaigns and fancy slogans to better position themselves. Unfortunately, you as the consumer are meant to weed through the policies to find the right one. Buying insurance should not be about buying the next product. Rather, it's about a strategy to buy into. It's not about trying to avoid wasting money; it's about how to waste money well. Hopefully, now, insurance will indeed make sense.

Author's Note

You will notice that in comparison to similar books, this one is quite short in length. The purpose of this is to help you, the reader, grasp the concept that follows without getting lost in complicated insurance jargon.

This book was created because there is nothing out there that offers a straightforward and practical guidance on how to purchase any insurance policy with confidence. However, around every corner, you will find another insurance product being touted as your fix all to life's problems. The bigger issue is that you're forced to sift through all those options yourself and then try to determine the best for your financial situation.

Unfortunately, there is one basic thing that is missing across all this, a fundamental strategy. When insurance is the only financial safety net you have to fall into, will it work for you the way you thought? Or will it leave you to pay for all the expensive realities that are sure to follow your worst possible day?

One critical thing the insurance industry at large does not tell you is this: insurance is *not* a product to buy. It is a strategy to buy into. Insurance products are commoditized. It is no different than buying ketchup at the grocery store. The problem is that in our society, we have a habit of buying insurance like we buy cars, cups of coffee, or any other consumable product. We buy it with the intention of using it. The biggest problem with that concept is you "never plan on anything bad happening to you." So why would a person need to have an insurance product at all? The only logical reason is based on the large financial impact of an unexpected event occurring. So the real challenge is how to break the mold of buying insurance based solely on the product and replace it with building a stronger financial strategy. I sincerely hope that small cost of this material, would prove to be good investment in better understanding insurance how you can apply it to your individual financial plan.

For more information and resources or to contact us, please visit insurancemakescents.com. Also, please feel free to leave a review or comment on the site where you purchased this material.

About the Author

It's been said that "life is the best classroom." We can learn many things from personal experiences and from those around us. Additionally, we often buy products based on those life lessons. As an author and entrepreneur, Nicholas is not immune to life teaching some of the most valuable lessons. Being in the insurance industry for well over a decade, Nicholas learned about a vital piece of missing information in the clouded industry of insurance. He then took the time developing the ideas that challenge the very fabric of how we buy insurance and presents them in his published book.

www.ingramcontent.com/pod-product-compliance
Lightning Source LLC
LaVergne TN
LVHW051058210926
848486LV00025B/425/J
* 9 7 9 8 8 9 4 2 7 3 3 1 0 *